weblinks

You don't need a computer to use this book. But, for readers who do have access to the Internet, the book provides links to recommended websites which offer additional information and resources on the subject.

You will find weblinks boxes like this on some pages of the book.

weblinks

For more information about Buddhism, go to www.waylinks.co.uk/series/21stcentury/Buddhism

waylinks.co.uk

To help you find the recommended websites easily and quickly, weblinks are provided on our own website, **waylinks.co.uk**. These take you straight to the relevant websites and save you typing in the Internet address yourself.

Internet safety

↗ Never give out personal details, which include: your name, address, school, telephone number, email address, password and mobile number.

↗ Do not respond to messages which make you feel uncomfortable – tell an adult.

↗ Do not arrange to meet in person someone you have met on the Internet.

↗ Never send your picture or anything else to an online friend without a parent's or teacher's permission.

↗ If you see anything that worries you, tell an adult.

A note to adults

Internet use by children should be supervised. We recommend that you install filtering software which blocks unsuitable material.

Website content

The weblinks for this book are checked and updated regularly. However, because of the nature of the Internet, the content of a website may change at any time, or a website may close down without notice. While the Publishers regret any inconvenience this may cause readers, they cannot be responsible for the content of any website other than their own.

HODDER
Wayland

21st Century
Buddhism

Anita Ganeri

HODDER
Wayland

an imprint of Hodder Children's Books

First published in 2005 by Hodder Wayland,
an imprint of Hodder Children's Books

© Hodder Wayland 2005

Consultant: The Clear Vision Trust (www.clear-vision.org)
Project Editor, Hodder Wayland: Kirsty Hamilton
Editor: Nicola Barber
Designer: Janet McCallum
Picture Researcher: Shelley Noronha, Glass Onion Pictures
Maps and artwork: Peter Bull

British Library Cataloguing Publication Data
Ganeri, Anita, 1961-
Buddhism – (21st century religions)
1. Buddhism – Juvenile literature
I. Title
294.3

ISBN 0750247053

Printed in China

Hodder Children's Books
A division of Hodder Headline Limited
338 Euston Road, London NW1 3BH

The publisher would like to thank the following for permission
to reproduce their pictures: Bridgeman Art Library
www.bridgeman.co.uk/ Ashmolean Museum/University of
Oxford 6, National Museum of India, New Delhi, India 18,
24; CIRCA Photo Library/William Holtby 16, 22, 44; Clear
Vision Trust 43; Corbis/Keren Su 29; Exile Images/N. Cooper
25, H. Davies 40; Robert Harding Picture Library 4, J.
Sweeney 10, A. Woolfitt 13, D. Traverso 15, G. Hellier 28, D.
Beatty 34, A. Woolfitt 35, U. Gahwiler 37; Hutchison Picture
Library 7, 19, 20, 33, 41; Ann and Bury Peerless 8, 9, 11, 17,
38, 39; Topfoto 21, 31, 36, 42, 45; ZUL 23, 27, 30, 32

Contents

Note

There are often two spellings for the key terms in Buddhism, depending on whether they are written in Pali or Sanskrit, two ancient languages of India. For example, the Pali word for the Buddha's teaching is Dhamma; the Sanskrit is Dharma. (Throughout this book, the most commonly known spelling is used.)

Introduction

Buddhism is one of the world's major religions. It began in northern India about 2,500 years ago when a royal prince, Siddhattha Gotama, first taught people how to free themselves from suffering. He became known as the Buddha, the Enlightened one or 'the One who knows the Truth'. Buddhists use his teachings, which they call the *Dhamma*, as a guide for their lives and as a path to an understanding of the way life is. (You can read a more detailed account of the Buddha's life in the next chapter.)

The Buddhist world

By the time of the Buddha's death, thousands of people in India had become his followers. Like him, many gave up their homes and possessions and became monks and nuns. They travelled around the country, teaching the Dhamma. From India, Buddhism spread all over Asia. In each country, it adapted to local customs and often mingled with local beliefs. Today, there are an estimated 400 million Buddhists. The population of some countries, such as Thailand, is mostly Buddhist. In other countries, Buddhists form the minority. More recently, Buddhism has become increasingly popular in Europe, North America and Australia.

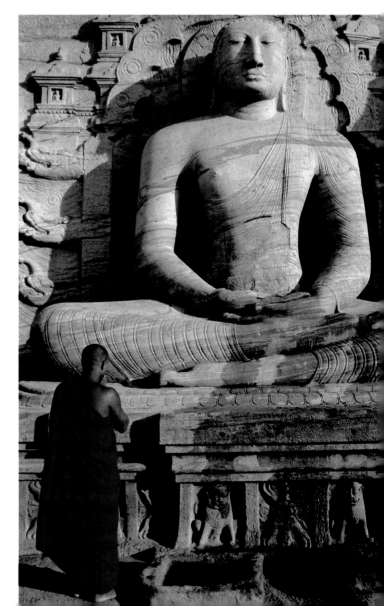

➤ *Buddhists honour the Buddha by bowing and making offerings to an image of the Buddha, as this monk in Sri Lanka is doing.*

4

The Buddha's teaching

Buddhism is unusual among the world's religions because it is not based on belief in a divine being, called God, who created the world and watches over it. The Buddha did not claim to be a god and did not expect to be worshipped as one. Rather, he was a human being who gained Enlightenment and understood the truth about life. Through his teaching, other people had the chance to achieve Enlightenment for themselves. However, the Buddha urged all his followers not to accept his teachings blindly, but to test them against their own experience.

Modern developments

Over the last two hundred years, Buddhism has faced many challenges, social, political and economic. In some parts of the world, materialism has weakened its influence. In others, Buddhists have been persecuted under harsh political regimes. Yet despite these challenges, Buddhist practices such as meditation are becoming a part of many people's everyday lives. So what does the future hold for Buddhism? A key Buddhist teaching states that everything is always changing. Nothing stays the same. It remains to be seen how Buddhism will cope with the changes it faces in the 21st century.

---
weblinks

For general information about many different aspects of Buddhism, go to
www.waylinks.co.uk/series/21stcentury/Buddhism

▼ *A map showing the estimated number of Buddhists in countries around the world today. Note: some countries such as Tibet have relatively small populations but their religion is still predominantly Buddhist.*

Estimated Buddhist population
- Over 10 million
- 1 - 10 million
- 100,000 - 1 million
- 5,000 - 100,000

1 History of Buddhism

According to tradition, Siddhattha Gotama was born in about 563BCE in Lumbini, in present-day Nepal. Our knowledge of Siddhattha comes partly from early sacred texts, and partly from later commentaries. Many legends also grew up around his life. These were recorded centuries after his death and may not be historically accurate.

Birth of the Buddha

According to the legends, Siddhattha was the son of King Suddodhana, the leader of the Shakya clan who lived in northeast India, on the border with Nepal. His mother was Queen Maya. One night, legend says, Queen Maya dreamt she was visited by a white elephant – a sign that she would have a baby who would grow into an exceptional person. Siddhattha was born on the full moon of May in a beautiful garden in Lumbini, Nepal.

Seven days later, Siddhattha's mother died and Siddhattha was brought up by his aunt in his father's luxurious palace. Here he was visited by an old wise man, called Asita, who foretold his future. Asita told the king that his son would grow up to be one of two things – a great ruler or a great teacher, depending on whether he ever stopped to think about suffering. Determined that Siddhattha should become a great ruler, the king tried to keep all knowledge of suffering from him. He kept him safe in the palace, surrounded by fine things. Guards were set around the palace to prevent him from seeing the outside world.

▼ *This stone carving shows the birth of the Buddha. It dates from the 2nd or 3rd centuries CE.*

As part of his upbringing, Siddhattha was taught the warrior skills he would need as a prince. At 16 years old, he was married to a princess from a neighbouring kingdom.

➤ *A tree festooned with prayer flags in the sacred garden in Lumbini, Nepal, where the Buddha is said to have been born. Written on the flags are Buddhist prayers which blow to all corners of the earth.*

Religion in India

The 6th century BCE, when Siddhattha was born, was a time of great religious change in India. Old ideas were being challenged and new ideas formulated. At the time, the main religion of India was a form of Hinduism (as it still is today). It is thought that Siddhattha may have been brought up as a Hindu, although no one knows for certain. As the Buddha, Siddhattha strongly criticized the Hindu priests who came from the Brahmin (upper) caste. They were seen as religious authorities and were very powerful. The Buddha taught that it was how people behaved, rather than the class into which they were born, that really mattered. According to the Buddha, the path to Enlightenment was open to everyone, whether rich or poor, high or low caste.

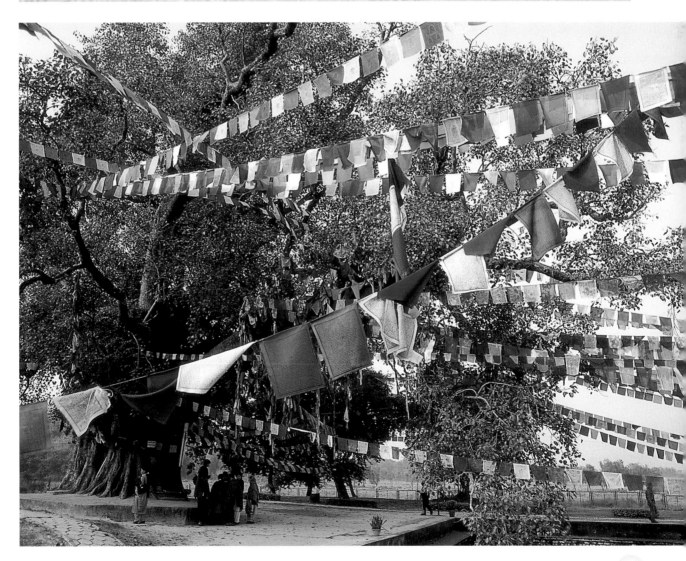

The Four Sights

Siddhattha lived very comfortably in his father's palace. But when he was 29 years old, he had an experience that changed his life. Disobeying his father's orders, he instructed his charioteer, Channa, to take him for a ride outside the palace walls. He was horrified by the grief and suffering he saw around him – a hunched old man, a sick man in great pain, and a corpse in a funeral procession. Channa explained that this was a normal part of life. Every day people grew old, fell ill and died. Then Siddhattha saw a holy man, dressed in a worn robe. The holy man had given up his home and possessions to search for a way to true happiness. He had nothing, but he looked deeply content.

That night, Siddhattha returned to the palace, his mind made up. He would leave his luxurious life behind and follow the example of the holy man. Secretly, he said goodbye to his wife and baby son, and left the palace. After riding all night, he came to the banks of a river where he cut off his long, black hair and exchanged his fine clothes for a simple robe. From now on, he would live as a wandering holy man, with no money, belongings or home.

▼ *This wall-painting from Thailand shows the Four Sights that Siddhattha saw on his chariot ride. They revealed to him that people suffered, grew old and died, as a normal part of life. On the right is the last of the Four Sights, the holy man.*

The search for Enlightenment

Siddhattha joined two religious teachers and learned how to meditate. Next, he spent six years in the forest with five other holy men. There Siddhattha lived a life of great hardship, believing that this would help him to become wiser. He wore rags, went for months on end without washing, spent long periods without moving, pulled out his hair and beard, and slept on a bed of thorns. But none of these practices helped him in his search for the truth. Finally, weak and exhausted, he left his companions and made his way to a village which is now known as Bodh Gaya. That evening, he sat under a tall bodhi tree and began to meditate.

During the night, legend says, Siddhattha was visited by Mara, the evil one, who tried to tempt him away from his search for the truth. But Siddhattha ignored the temptation, continued to meditate, and Mara fled.

As the night drew on, Siddhattha finally found the answers he had been looking for. Suddenly, he saw the truth about why people suffered and how he could help them. He now became the Buddha, the Enlightened or awakened one.

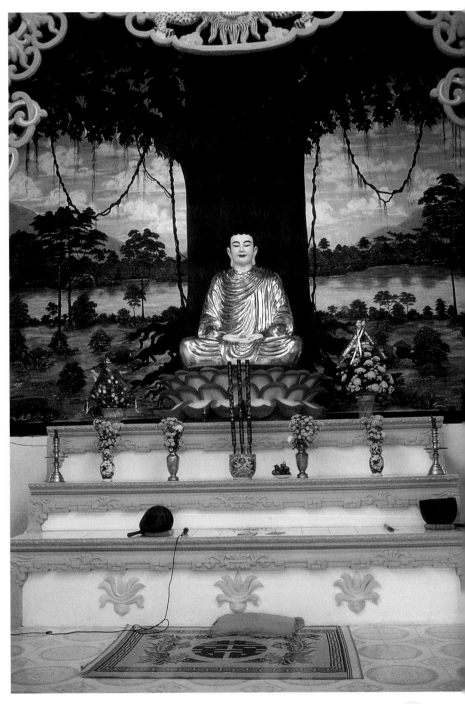

► *An image from a temple in Vietnam of Siddhattha meditating under the bodhi tree. Many Buddhists temples and viharas have statues like this one to remind people of the story of the Buddha's Enlightenment.*

The first teaching

After his Enlightenment, the Buddha continued to meditate for many more days and nights. He was filled with a great sense of peace and happiness. During this time, he received his first two followers. These were two passing merchants who gave him food. Determined to teach other people what he had discovered, the Buddha made his way to the Deer Park at Sarnath where he found the five holy men who had been his companions in the forest (see page 9). To them, he gave his first teaching, in which he explained the cause of suffering (see page 16). His words were so convincing and powerful that the holy men quickly gained Enlightenment. They then formally pledged to follow the Buddha and his teachings.

Travelling and teaching

For the next forty-five years, the Buddha travelled around northeast India, teaching people from all walks of life. His followers – monks, nuns and laypeople – became known as the *Sangha*, or Buddhist community.

▼ *The Dhamekh Stupa in Sarnath, India, is said to stand on the very spot where the Buddha gave his first teaching after his Enlightenment. It is an important place of pilgrimage for Buddhists.*

During this time, the Buddha helped many other people to achieve Enlightenment. They became known as *arahats*, or 'worthy ones', and were sent out by the Buddha to teach. The year after his Enlightenment, the Buddha returned home to visit his family. He was reconciled with his father, who became an arahat, and his aunt, who became the first nun. He also ordained his young son, Rahula, as a monk.

Passing away

When the Buddha was about 80 years old, he fell ill with food poisoning and knew that his life was drawing to an end. He told his faithful companion, Ananda, not to look for another leader when he was gone but to let the Dhamma be a guide for his followers. Then he called the monks together and made

▲ *This carved stone statue from Sri Lanka shows the Buddha's parinirvana. Legend says that the Buddha lay on his right-hand side when he passed away and that an earthquake shook the earth.*

his last journey to the village of Kushinagara. Just outside the town, he stopped in a grove of trees where he lay down to rest. His last words were to remind the monks of the teaching that everything changes and passes away. Then he died. This event is known as the *parinirvana*, which means the final extinction of greed, hatred and ignorance.

After the Buddha's death, the monks held a ceremony in his honour which lasted for six days. Then his body was cremated. His ashes were divided into eight parts and given to the rulers of eight different clans. Dome-shaped burial monuments, called *stupas*, were built over them (see page 28).

11

Buddhism splits

During the Buddha's life, his teachings were not written down. Instead, they were memorized by his followers and passed on by word of mouth. Shortly after his death, it is said that a council of monks was called to collect all the teachings together. However, nothing was written down until several centuries later. Soon different opinions began to arise among the various groups of monks about what the Buddha had actually taught. These disagreements became stronger at a second council, held about fifty to a hundred years after the Buddha's death. The main disagreement was over the rules about how monks and nuns should live. Subsequently, Buddhism split into two groups – *Theravada*, or 'the way of the elders', and *Mahayana*, or 'the great way'. (You can read more about them on page 18.)

Buddhism spreads

Despite the split between the two groups, Buddhism continued to spread very quickly in India and throughout the rest of Asia. Theravada Buddhism spread south and east to Sri Lanka, Myanmar (Burma), Cambodia, Laos and Thailand. It reached Sri Lanka in

▼ *This map shows how the two main schools of Buddhism – Mayahana and Theravada – spread out of India and became established in other countries around the world.*

Korea

Japan

C h i n a

Tibet

Nepal

Bodh Gaya

I n d i a

Myanmar

Laos

Vietnam

Thailand

Cambodia

Sri Lanka

→ The spread of Buddhism

Mahayana Buddhism

Theravada Buddhism

about 250BCE, when the son of Emperor Ashoka (see box) converted the king and most of the islanders. Mahayana Buddhism spread north and west to Nepal, Tibet, China, Japan, Vietnam and Korea. Buddhism first reached China in the 1st century CE, along the trade route known as the Silk Road. However, by the 12th century CE, Buddhism had almost disappeared from India, its original home. Two factors may have caused its decline – its merger with local religions, and the fact that its peaceful nature made it vulnerable to the military might of invaders, such as the Muslim Mughal rulers of northern India.

Emperor Ashoka

The great Indian emperor, Ashoka Maurya, came to the throne in 268BCE. Through a series of military campaigns he quickly expanded his empire to include most of India, apart from the southern tip. After one particularly bloody battle, in which 100,000 people were killed, Ashoka was filled with remorse for the suffering his greed had caused. He vowed to set up a society based not on violence but on the Buddhist principles of peace and compassion. All over his empire, he erected pillars on which decrees were carved, telling people to live just, truthful and generous lives. Ashoka himself tried to set an example. He established hospitals for the poor, and built wells and reservoirs. He also sent missionaries, including his own son and daughter, far and wide to spread the Buddha's teachings.

➤ *The famous lion capital (top) from Ashoka's pillar in Sarnath, India. The four back-to-back lions were Ashoka's symbols and represented bravery. They are now the state symbol of modern India.*

2 Beliefs and sacred texts

Despite differences in how they interpret the Buddha's teachings and practise their faith, the different groups of Buddhists share the same basic beliefs. For example, Buddhists believe that when a person dies, he or she is born again in a different form – a human body, a plant or an animal. This is also called reincarnation. The Buddha's teachings are set down and explained in the Buddhist sacred texts. Unlike other religions, such as Islam and Christianity, Buddhism does not have just one main sacred text. Each group of Buddhists follows its own set of scriptures.

The turning of the wheel

In the first teaching he gave, to the five holy men, the Buddha explained that life was like a wheel in which everyone was caught, endlessly turning in a cycle of birth, death and rebirth. What kept the wheel turning was *karma* – actions and their consequences. This meant that people's future happiness depended on the way they behaved. The only way to escape this endless cycle of birth and death was to move towards *nirvana*, or Enlightenment. By behaving kindly and wisely a person would move nearer to Enlightenment, while selfishness and unkindness would lead him or her further away from Enlightenment.

Three Marks of Being

Another crucial part of the Buddha's teachings is called the Three Marks of Being. These are *dukkha*, *anicca* and *anatta*. Everything the Buddha taught is based on these three signs.

1 Dukkha is a Pali word which means 'that which is difficult to bear'. It can mean suffering physical illness or pain, but it also includes feelings of boredom and frustration, and awareness of other people's suffering.

2 Anicca means 'impermanence'. This means that everything is constantly changing and nothing lasts for ever. Plants and animals die. Loved ones pass away. Even seemingly solid rocks and mountains slowly erode and crumble away.

3 Anatta means 'no fixed self'. Many religions believe a person has a soul or spirit which lives on after the death of the body. However, the Buddha taught that if we look at our own experience we will see that everything about us is always changing, including our emotions and thoughts. Therefore there cannot be anything about us that is fixed or permanent, including our own self.

The five parts of a person

The Buddha taught that human beings are made up of five parts or elements, called *skandhas*. The word skandha means 'bundle'.

The five elements are: form (our physical bodies); sensation (our feelings); perception (our senses); determination (our thoughts); and consciousness (our awareness).

The way in which all five of these elements come together changes with each rebirth, and is what makes everyone different.

▼ *This painting from Tibet shows Yama, the Lord of Death, holding the Wheel of Life. It represents the cycle of birth, death and rebirth. Around the outside of the wheel are the different stages of a person's life. Inside are some of the various ways in which a person might be reborn. The three animals in the middle stand for confusion, greed and hatred. These must be overcome in order to achieve Enlightenment.*

The Four Noble Truths

In the second part of his teaching, the Buddha explained why people feel dissatisfied with their lives and how they can rise above this dissatisfaction to find happiness. This teaching is called the Four Noble Truths:

1 Everyone experiences dukkha, or suffering, in life.

2 Suffering is caused by people's greed, selfishness and lack of contentment with what they have.

3 There is a way to end suffering.

4 The way to end suffering is to follow the Noble Eightfold Path.

The Noble Eightfold Path

In his life, the Buddha experienced both luxury and great hardship, and he knew that neither led to happiness. He taught the Noble Eightfold Path, a middle path for people to take between those two extremes. The Path shows eight ways in which people should live:

1 Right understanding – seeing through experience that the Buddha's teaching about life is true.

2 Right intention – having compassion for other people and thinking about people in a kind, generous way.

3 Right speech – not telling lies, swearing or speaking harshly but using words that are helpful and kind. In some cases, it is better to stay silent if you cannot think of something useful to say.

4 Right action – treating other people well and not doing anything to harm them, such as killing or stealing.

▼ *This group of images in a temple in Myanmar shows the Buddha teaching the Four Noble Truths during his first teaching in the Deer Park in Sarnath.*

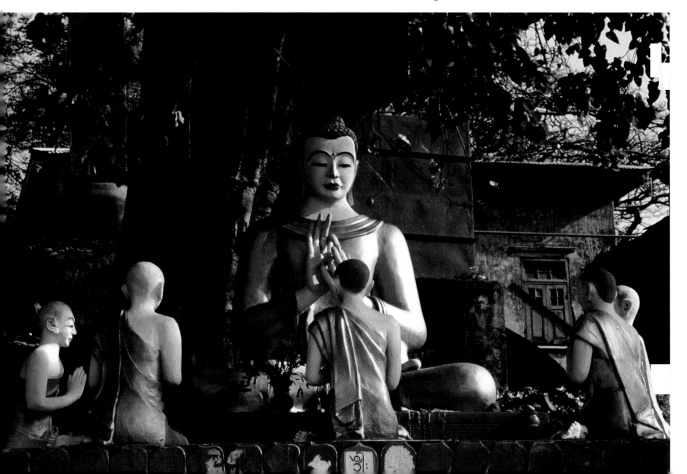

5 Right livelihood – earning your living doing something that helps the world and does not harm other people or animals.

6 Right effort – making an effort to do your best to be kind and avoid doing harm.

7 Right mindfulness – being calm and aware of your actions, feelings and thoughts.

8 Right concentration – training your mind to be calm and peaceful through meditation.

Nirvana

Nirvana is the Buddhist term for the perfect peace and happiness entered when the circle of birth, death and rebirth is broken, and all suffering ends. The word literally means 'blown out'. In a Buddhist story, a house is burning with three fires of hatred, greed and ignorance, causing great unhappiness. Following the Dhamma helps to blow the fires out. When all three fires are extinguished, suffering ends and there is nirvana.

In our own words

"Nirvana, or Enlightenment, is a way of experiencing life. If, one day, I become free from greed, hatred and ignorance and can see things just as they are, I'll be positive whatever happens. I won't expect things to last, or to make me happy, so I won't suffer when they don't! As I am now, I may feel happy when I have cake in front of me, and a bit sad when it rains. But if I were Enlightened, my mood wouldn't depend on what was going on at the time, so I'd be emotionally free. What a relief!"

Munisha, Member of the Western Buddhist Order, UK

◄ The eight-spoked Dhamma wheel is an important symbol in Buddhism. The spokes stand for the eight steps on the Noble Eightfold Path.

Theravada and Mahayana

All Buddhists follow the teachings of the Buddha, but they interpret and practise these teachings in different ways. Theravada Buddhists follow the Buddha and study the earliest scriptures in which his teachings are recorded. Mahayana Buddhists follow later Enlightened Buddhist teachers as well as the Buddha himself, and they have additional, later scriptures. They also worship mythical, heroic figures known as *bodhisattvas* (see box below).

Bodhisattvas

The word bodhisattva means a 'being of Enlightenment'. According to Mahayana belief, a bodhisattva is a mythical, heroic figure who has gained Enlightenment and become a Buddha. Out of compassion, bodhisattvas choose to help other people to overcome suffering. Selflessly, they put the happiness of other beings in the world before their own, and people pray to them for help and guidance. There are thousands of bodhisattvas. One of the most popular is Avalokiteshvara who represents perfect compassion. His name means 'the Lord who looks down'. He is often depicted with a thousand arms which show that he is ready to help everyone at once. He also has eleven heads and a thousand eyes to help him see all suffering beings. Mayahana Buddhists believe that we can all become more like bodhisattvas: full of kindness and concern for the world.

➤ This Tibetan painting shows the bodhisattva, Avalokiteshvara. He is worshipped, especially in Tibet, for his great compassion and care for those who are suffering.

Zen Buddhism

One of the best-known branches of Mahayana Buddhism, Zen, is practised mainly in Japan and China. It has also become popular in the West. According to tradition, an Indian monk called Bodhidharma introduced Zen into China in the 5th century CE. The word Zen means 'meditation' or 'contemplation' and Zen Buddhists emphasize meditation as a way to experience the truth behind all things and see the world as it really is. Learning to meditate can take many years, but Zen Buddhists use different techniques to help them see life more clearly, including painting, writing poetry, gardening and martial arts such as karate. These are all seen as ways of reaching directly into reality.

Tibetan Buddhism

Buddhism reached Tibet from India in the 7th century CE when the Tibetan king's two Buddhist wives encouraged him to convert. A long struggle followed between Buddhism and Bon, the ancient Tibetan religion. By the 14th century, however, Buddhism had become the country's main religion. Tibetan Buddhism is a mixture of Mahayana and Tantric beliefs and it includes many colourful rites and rituals to help on the path to Enlightenment. (Tantric Buddhism is based on a set of mysterious texts that describe rituals, magic and meditation techniques.) Many bodhisattvas are worshipped, including Avalokiteshvara. Today, Tibetan Buddhism faces an uncertain future, following the Chinese takeover of the country (see page 43).

▼ A Zen monk, dressed in his traditional black robes, in a monastery in Japan. Zen monks undergo very strict training in meditation.

Buddhism in daily life

All Buddhists try to follow the example of the Buddha's life and to live by his teachings in everything they do. This means cultivating the qualities of wisdom, loving compassion and morality. Buddhists believe that if they are kind, generous, truthful, helpful and patient they will suffer less, cause less suffering, and help others suffer less. They also believe that people are naturally kind and wise, but because they don't understand the truth about life, they often behave unkindly. People think that things will make them happy, and they keep wanting things – trying to hold on to them and keep them the same. This makes people selfish and greedy. However, Buddhism teaches its followers to accept that things are always changing. As people become kinder, wiser and more contented with what they have got, they gradually move nearer to Enlightenment: perfect compassion and contentment with life as it is.

▼ *A monk meditates under a tree in Lumbini, the birthplace of the Buddha. Buddhists try to follow the example of the Buddha in all aspects of their lives.*

The Three Jewels

In their daily lives, Buddhists commit themselves to the Three Jewels of Buddhism. These are the Buddha himself, as a great teacher and as the symbol of everyone's potential to gain Enlightenment; the Dhamma, the Buddha's teaching; and the Sangha, the community of Buddhist laypeople, monks and nuns. These are called jewels, or treasures, because they are so precious. Every day, Buddhists show that they place their trust in the Three Jewels by reciting these words:

> 'I go for refuge to the Buddha
> I go for refuge to the Dhamma
> I go for refuge to the Sangha.'

The Five Moral Precepts

Buddhists also follow a set of guidelines, called the Five Moral Precepts. They undertake:

1 Not to kill or harm living beings.

2 Not to steal or take things which are not freely given.

3 To avoid sexual misconduct.

4 Not to speak unkindly or tell lies.

5 Not to drink alcohol or take drugs that might cloud the mind.

Each Precept also has a positive side. For example, it is not enough to avoid harming living beings. You should actively show kindness and compassion. The Five Positives are to develop loving kindness, generosity, contentment, kindly and truthful speech, and mindfulness or clear awareness.

➤ *A Japanese Buddhist prays for peace during a vigil in Union Square, New York, USA after the terrorist attacks of 11 September 2001.*

In our own words

"*Every day, I try to remember that everything I do, think and say has an effect on me and others. I meditate for about 45 minutes before breakfast. It helps me notice how I am feeling. If I know I'm in a bad mood, I can be careful not to take it out on others. I try to speak kindly, even when disagreeing with someone, and I recycle or compost as much of my rubbish as possible so as to lessen my effect on our world. I love humour, and the thing I have had to work hardest at is not making insensitive and hurtful jokes. I can't be perfect, but I try my best, and apologize when I slip up.*"

Munisha, Member of the Western Buddhist Order, UK

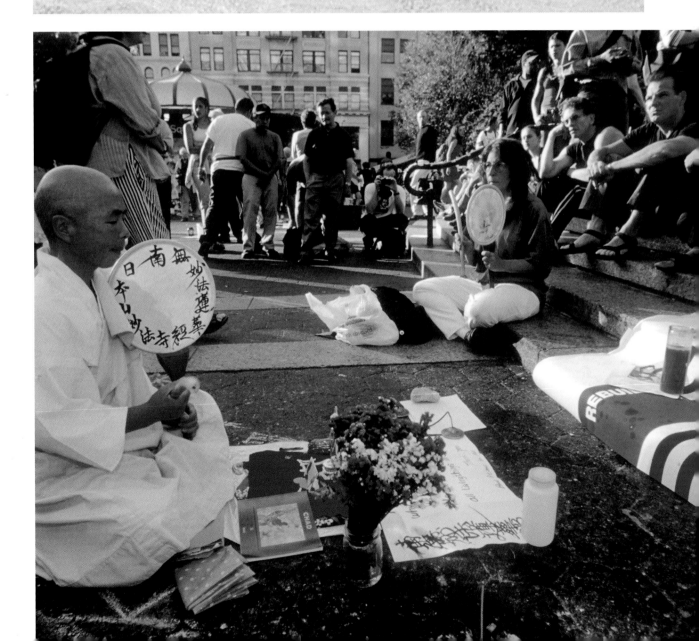

Sacred texts

There are hundreds of sacred texts in Buddhism, linked to the various traditions and schools. Some texts contain the teachings of the Buddha; others are commentaries or writings by later Buddhist monks and teachers. Chanting from the sacred texts is an important part of Buddhist practice. Monks and nuns study the texts and help laypeople to understand their meaning.

Collecting the texts

For centuries after the Buddha's death, monks learned his teachings by heart and passed them on by word of mouth. Groups of monks met regularly to recite the teachings so that they did not forget them. In the 1st century BCE, as the numbers of monks fell, the teachings were finally written down in Pali,

an ancient Indian language. These texts became the sacred texts of the Theravada Buddhists. Later texts were written down in Sanskrit, another ancient and sacred Indian language. Because of this, two spellings – the Pali and the Sanskrit – are often given for Buddhist words. For example, nirvana is the Sanskrit word; in Pali, it is spelt nibbana.

The Tipitaka

The sacred texts of the Theravada Buddhists are called the *Tipitaka* which means 'Three

▼ *This painting from Myanmar shows a scene from a Buddhist story called a* Jataka. *The* Jatakas *are part of the* Tipitaka *and tell the stories of the Buddha's past lives. In this story, 'The Goodness of the Elephant King', the Buddha appears as an elephant to teach about generosity and gratitude.*

▲ *Some pages from a copy of the* Tipitaka. *The text is written in Pali on palm leaves, shaped into rectangular pages to copy the format that was used when the* Tipitaka *was first recorded.*

Baskets'. This is because the texts were first written down on palm leaves, stored in three collections or 'baskets'. The first 'basket', the *Vinaya Pitaka*, sets out the rules laid down by the Buddha for how monks and nuns should live. The second 'basket' is the *Sutta Pitaka* which contains discourses by the Buddha on the key teachings of Buddhism. The third 'basket', the *Abhi Dhamma Pitaka*, is made up of commentaries which help to explain the Buddha's teachings. The *Tipitaka* is also known as the *Pali Canon*.

---
weblinks

For more information about Buddhist sacred texts and some of the *Jataka* stories from the *Tipitaka*, go to
www.waylinks.co.uk/series/21stcentury/Buddhism

The Metta Sutta

The Metta Sutta *is found in the* Sutta Pitaka, *the second basket of the* Tipitaka. *It is a famous discourse, or talk, given by the Buddha, on the importance of metta, or loving kindness. It is recited as part of everyday Buddhist practice by monks and laypeople. This is part of the* Metta Sutta:

'May all beings be well and happy, may their hearts be whole and pure! Whatever living beings there be – Weak or strong, tall or short, Small or large, seen or unseen, Living far or near, those who are Born and those yet to be born – May all beings, without exception, be happy!'

Mahayana Scriptures

Mahayana Buddhists have their own sacred texts, called 'sutras'. Most of these texts were originally written down in Sanskrit from about the 1st century CE, and were later translated into Chinese, Tibetan and Japanese. For Mahayana Buddhists, some of these texts are believed to be the genuine word of the Buddha. Others were written by later Enlightened teachers; some have no author. They were considered so precious that, centuries ago, monks made long and dangerous journeys to obtain copies of them from India.

The Lotus Sutra

The *Lotus Sutra* is one of the most popular Mahayana texts, especially in Japan and China. This sutra is in the form of a talk given by the Buddha to a huge gathering of followers and bodhisattvas. In it, the Buddha puts forward the key Mahayana belief that everyone has the potential to gain Enlightenment. To explain this idea, the Buddha compares himself to a rain cloud which rains down on all plants, large and small. In the same way, the Buddha 'rains down' the Dhamma and everyone may benefit in their own way.

▼ *This is a page from the* Diamond Sutra, *one of the most important Mahayana sacred texts. It shows the Buddha teaching his elderly follower, the monk Subhuti. This copy was made in China in 868CE.*

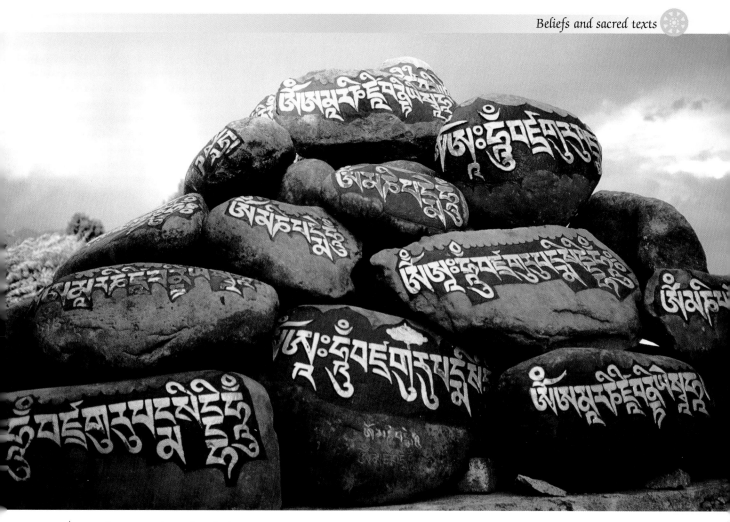

▲ *In Tibet, sacred words called mantras are painted or carved on to prayer stones.*

The Diamond Sutra

The *Diamond Sutra* is a short text of about 300 verses which forms part of a collection of texts called the *Sutras of Perfect Wisdom*. 'Perfect Wisdom' means gaining a full and complete insight into how things really are. The *Diamond Sutra* was composed in about 300CE and translated into Tibetan and Chinese. Its main teaching is that nothing exists by itself – everything is interconnected. This is why nothing in the world is fixed or everlasting. Like a diamond which is hard enough to cut through other materials, the *Diamond Sutra* is thought to have the power to cut through ignorance for those who study it carefully.

Tibetan texts

The sacred texts of the Tibetan Buddhists are translations of Indian writings, collected between the 7th and 14th centuries CE. The texts are divided into two sections – the *Kanjur* and the *Tenjur*. The *Kanjur*, or 'Word of the Buddha', contains more than 1,000 texts of the Buddha's teachings. The *Tenjur*, or 'Treatises', contains some 3,000 treatises and commentaries on the teachings. Another famous Tibetan text is the *Bardo Thodrol*, or *Tibetan Book of the Dead*. When a person is dying, a monk reads to them from this book. The words are intended to guide the person safely through Bardo, a world between death and rebirth.

3 Practice, places of worship and holy days

Some Western Buddhists do not like to use the word 'worship' to describe how they express their beliefs because they feel it implies worship of God or a god. They prefer 'practice' instead, or *puja*, an Indian word for ritual or prayer. Buddhist practice varies around the world but usually includes honouring the Buddha at home or in the *vihara*, and observing festivals and other holy days. For many Buddhists, this is a way of gaining 'merit' which will help to ensure that their next lives are good ones. When they worship, they acknowledge what is most valuable in life, and resolve to follow it. They believe that this will lessen their suffering in this life as well as in possible future lives.

Visiting a vihara

A vihara is a Buddhist temple or monastery. The earliest viharas were simple huts, built by the Buddha's first followers. The monks stayed in them during the rainy season when the weather made it difficult for them to travel. Buddhists may visit the vihara at any time, although many have set times for puja, conducted by the monks. After entering the shrine room, Buddhists kneel and bow three times in front of the image of the Buddha installed there. The three bows represent the Buddha, the Dhamma and the Sangha. Then the worshippers repeat their commitment to the Three Jewels and recite the Five Moral Precepts (see page 20).

Making offerings

As part of Buddhist practice, people may place offerings of flowers, candles and incense in front of the Buddha's image. Each offering has a special significance. Fresh flowers will eventually droop and die, a reminder that nothing lasts for ever. Candles light up a room just as the Buddha's teaching lights up people's lives. And like the Dhamma, the sweet smell of incense spreads everywhere, reminding Buddhists that even their smallest actions have an effect. These offerings are accompanied by chanting. For example:

'Offerings to the Buddha.
Reverencing the Buddha, we offer flowers –
Flowers that today are fresh and sweetly
  blooming,
Flowers that tomorrow are faded and fallen.
Our bodies too, like flowers, will pass away.

Reverencing the Buddha, we offer candles.
To him, who is the light, we offer light.
From his greater lamp a lesser lamp we light
  within us:
The lamp of bodhi shining within our hearts.

Reverencing the Buddha, we offer incense.
Incense whose fragrance pervades the air.
The fragrance of the perfect life, sweeter than
   incense,
Spreads in all directions throughout the world.'

(Puja: the FWBO book of Buddhist devotional texts ©
Windhorse Publications 1999. Offerings to the Buddha
from The Threefold Puja page 35.)

---

weblinks

For more information about places of worship, go to
www.waylinks.co.uk/series/21stcentury/Buddhism

▼ *Children at a vihara in London, UK, show their respect for the Buddha by
leaving offerings in front of his image.*

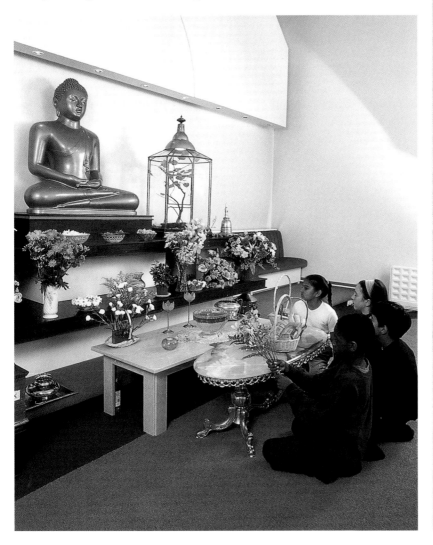

Meditation

Meditation is central to Buddhist practice. Buddhists believe that through training their minds they can overcome their ignorance, greed and hatred, and understand the true nature of things. The Buddha himself gained Enlightenment while meditating. Meditation is also linked to three steps on the Noble Eightfold Path – right effort, right mindfulness and right concentration. Through meditation, a person can quiet or still the mind in order to experience inner peace. Learning to meditate, however, takes time and it is important to have a good teacher. It is also important to find a suitable place and time. Many Buddhists meditate every day, on their own or in a group. There are many different kinds of meditation but often Buddhists sit in a quiet room, eyes closed, and rest their attention on their breathing.

Places of worship

Buddhist places of worship vary in style, depending on the country and particular Buddhist group. Traditionally they are purpose-built, but in many Western countries, Buddhists have converted old buildings into temples. The stupa provided the earliest focus of worship in Buddhism. After the death of the Buddha, his ashes were divided and placed in stupas in various parts of northern India. Today, these dome-shaped funeral mounds are found all over the Buddhist world, many containing the relics of great Buddhist teachers. They vary in shape from country to country, for example in China and Japan most stupas are pagodas. When visiting a stupa, Buddhists may walk round it clockwise many times. As they walk they may also chant *mantras*, or sacred verses, in honour of the Buddha and his teaching.

◀ *The striking white dome of the Swayambunath stupa in Kathmandu, Nepal. No one is sure exactly when the stupa was built, but by the 1200s it had become an important Buddhist centre.*

▲ *A Buddhist pilgrim at the Jokhang Temple in Lhasa, Tibet. He is standing next to a row of giant prayer wheels which he spins as he passes, in order to release the prayers.*

Places of pilgrimage

Many Buddhists like to make pilgrimages to sacred stupas, shrines and places associated with the Buddha's life. For Tibetan Buddhists, the holiest site is the Jokhang Temple in Lhasa. Built in the 7th century CE, legend has it that the temple stands on the site of a great underground lake in which people could see their future. On entering the temple, pilgrims pass rows of huge prayer wheels before reaching the main hall which contains an ancient bronze image of the Buddha, sitting on top of a golden throne.

There are also shrines dedicated to Avalokiteshvara and other bodhisattvas. Outside the temple, the flagstones have been worn smooth by thousands of pilgrims prostrating themselves on the ground to show their respect for the Buddha.

weblinks▶

For more information about the Jokhang Temple in Lhasa, Tibet, go to www.waylinks.co.uk/series/21stcentury/Buddhism

Art and symbolism

Buddhist artists have created exquisite statues, paintings and carvings. But Buddhist art is not simply decorative. Its purpose is to remind, support and reinforce the Buddha's teachings. The earliest works were cave paintings and carvings, showing scenes from the Buddha's life. For hundreds of years after his death, the Buddha was not shown in person. Instead, he was represented by symbols, such as a bodhi tree (for Enlightenment), footprints (for his travels), or a wheel (for the Dhamma). In scenes of his past lives, he was shown as a deer or other animal. The first images of the Buddha appeared by the 1st century CE.

➤ *A modern image of the Buddha from a temple in Sri Lanka, showing his long earlobes and curled hair.*

Buddha images

Buddhists do not actually worship images of the Buddha. The images represent the possibility of Enlightenment, the Buddha's teachings and his special qualities, such as tranquillity and compassion. They inspire Buddhists to remember these qualities and develop them within themselves. Images show a variety of ancient signs that mark the Buddha out as an extraordinary human being. These include long earlobes, tightly curled hair, and lotus or wheel signs on the soles of his feet. In Mahayana Buddhism, there are also many images of bodhisattvas. They can be identified by the symbolic objects they carry, such as lotus flowers or diamond thunderbolts.

Mudras

In images of the Buddha and bodhisattvas, hands and fingers are portrayed being held in special, symbolic gestures, called *mudras*. Mudra is a Sanskrit word, meaning 'sign' or 'seal'. In the *abhaya* (fearlessness) mudra, one hand is raised, with its palm facing forward, in a sign of protection and reassurance. In the *dharmachakra* (wheel-turning) mudra, both hands are held together to symbolize the teaching of the Dhamma. The *dhyana* (meditation) mudra is a sign of meditation, with both hands resting in the lap. In the *bhumisparsha* (earth-touching) mudra, the Buddha touches the earth with one hand, just as he did at his Enlightenment (see page 9).

Mandalas

A mandala *is a circular, symbolic picture map showing the way to Enlightenment. It is used by Tibetan Buddhists to focus their minds for meditation. Around the outside is a protective ring of flames to burn impurities such as greed, hatred and ignorance. A second ring of thunderbolts shows the indestructible nature of Enlightenment. A final ring of lotus flowers symbolizes the purity of the land the meditating person is entering. Inside, there are four open gateways leading to the centre. Here, there stands a picture of a bodhisattva representing a quality, such as wisdom or compassion. As a person meditates on the mandala, his or her mind moves through the different parts of the picture to reach the centre of the mandala – Enlightenment, freedom from suffering.*

▼ *This mandala has been made from coloured sand by Tibetan monks. The mandala will later be destroyed at a special ceremony. This is a reminder of the Buddha's teaching that nothing lasts for ever.*

Buddhist festivals

Many Buddhist festivals are celebrated during the year. The majority are associated with events from the Buddha's life, such as his birth, Enlightenment and parinirvana, the lives of great Buddhist teachers or major episodes in Buddhist history. Some are observed by Buddhists everywhere; others are special to particular groups. Celebrations vary from country to country, and are influenced by local customs and traditions. Many festivals fall at the time of the full moon because, traditionally, this is when the key events in the Buddha's life are said to have happened. This is also when the monks traditionally met to recite the Dhamma and rules of the monastic order (see page 36).

Wesak

For Theravada Buddhists and many others, the most important festival of the year is Wesak. It takes place on the full moon day of April or May and celebrates the Buddha's Enlightenment. Some Buddhists remember his birth and death on this day too. To mark Wesak, people may decorate their homes and viharas with lamps and candles which represent the light of Enlightenment. They may also visit the vihara for a special Wesak puja and to take gifts for the monks. Many Buddhists exchange Wesak cards, decorated with symbols such as lotus flowers or Dhamma wheels.

The sacred tooth

A Theravada festival, Asala, occurs in July or August. It commemorates the first talk given by the Buddha after his Enlightenment. In Kandy, Sri Lanka, a series of spectacular processions, or *peraheras*, takes place through the streets. At the height of the festival, there is a parade of beautifully decorated elephants, accompanied by dancers, drummers and musicians. Carried on the back of one of the

▼ *A huge, illuminated Wesak decoration from Sri Lanka. It shows the chariot in which Siddhattha rode when he saw the Four Sights.*

elephants is a replica of a golden casket. The original is kept safely in the nearby Temple of the Tooth. It contains a very precious relic, said to be one of the Buddha's own teeth.

Hana Matsuri

The festival of Hana Matsuri is a very important one for Mahayana Buddhists in Japan. Celebrated in April, the festival marks the birth of the Buddha. It is also a flower festival, celebrating the coming of spring. ('Hana' is Japanese for flower; 'matsuri' means festival.) At Hana Matsuri, model flower gardens are set up in the courtyards of Buddhist temples, as reminders of the garden in which the Buddha is believed to have been born. Images of the baby Buddha are placed in the gardens. Visitors pour spoonfuls of scented tea over the images, to remember the story of the scented water sent by the gods to bathe the Buddha at his birth.

▲ *Children in Japan dress up to celebrate the Hana Matsuri festival. They are wearing flowers in their hair to honour the Buddha.*

weblinks

For more information about a variety of Buddhist festivals, go to
www.waylinks.co.uk/series/21stcentury/Buddhism

In our own words

"On the day of Wesak, I usually take the day off work. I spend some time relaxing at home and the rest at the Buddhist Centre with my friends. At the Centre, some of us meditate together. In the evening, loads of people meet there, some of them with their children. We all bring vegetarian food for a big shared meal, and then we go up to the shrine hall. There's usually a talk about the meaning of the Buddha's Enlightenment, and then we *have a special puja, or ritual, to celebrate his life and remind ourselves that we are trying to follow his example. There is lots of chanting and readings and people light candles and incense in front of the Buddha figure. The small children play and run up and down the corridor when they get bored!"*

Munisha, Member of the Western Buddhist Order, UK

4 Monks and monasteries

The Buddha spent a large part of his life living as a wandering holy man and teaching the Dhamma. Following in his footsteps, some devout Buddhists leave their homes and belongings, and dedicate their lives to learning and practising the Buddha's teachings. They form the monastic Sangha, or community, of monks (*bhikkhus*) and nuns (*bhikkhunis*).

Becoming a monk

In many Theravada countries, young boys spend several months in a monastery as part of their education. Some then leave and return to their families and the outside world. Others stay on in the monastery and are ordained as monks. In Sri Lanka, the ordination ceremony dates back to the time of the Buddha. First, the young monk has his head (and beard) shaved. This is a sign that he is no longer living an everyday life. Then he bathes as a symbol of his desire to live a purer life. He kneels in front of the senior monk present and asks permission to wear his

▼ *Boys in Sri Lanka being ordained as Buddhist monks. They are kneeling in front of the senior monks and holding their new robes.*

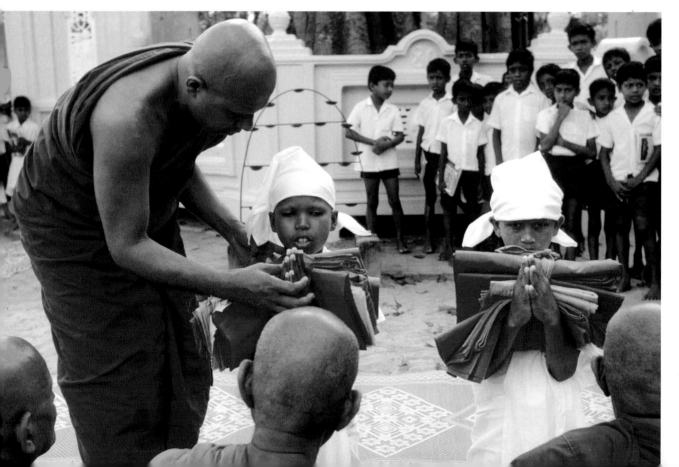

yellow monk's robes and to be ordained. (In Tibet and Myanmar, monks' robes are maroon. In Japan, they are black.) He also begs forgiveness for his faults, and pledges his commitment to the Three Jewels. If the monks consider him suitable, he is accepted as a bhikkhu.

The Eight Requisites

In order to be detached from worldly ties, Buddhist monks and nuns have very few personal possessions. Traditionally, since the Buddha's time, they have only been allowed to own eight items which are absolutely necessary, called the Eight Requisites. These are three robes, an alms bowl, a belt, a water-strainer, a walking stick, a toothpick, a needle, and a razor (for monks). Everything else they use belongs to the monastery.

Western orders

The Friends of the Western Buddhist Order is one of the best-known new Buddhist groups in Western countries (see page 44). Women and men who join the Order itself are known as 'Order Members'. Although they make a serious commitment to the Dhamma, they do not become monks or nuns. For example, they do not live in monasteries or rely on the local community for food, as is traditional for monks in many Buddhist countries. Some teach and run Buddhist centres. Others have ordinary jobs or work in businesses which promote 'right livelihood' (see page 17), such as running bookshops which sell books about Buddhism, or cafes which serve vegetarian food. They may have partners and children, and they may live in Buddhist communities or in their own homes.

▼ *These women are being ordained as Buddhist nuns in Britain in a monastery that follows the Theravada tradition.*

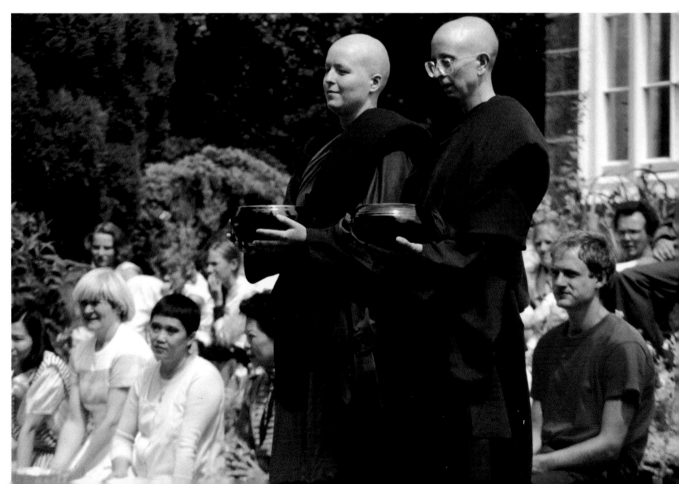

Rules for monks and nuns

Monks and nuns must follow strict rules of discipline, called the *vinaya*, set down by the Buddha. The vinaya is one of the three baskets of the *Tipitaka* (see page 23). It sets out the rules, then explains when and in what circumstances they were devised and gives examples. Many monasteries have 227 rules but the number can vary in some Mahayana groups. These rules include the Ten Moral Precepts, which are the Five Moral Precepts followed by lay Buddhists (see page 20) plus five other rules: not eating after midday, not singing or dancing in a frivolous way, not wearing jewellery or perfume, not sleeping on a soft bed, and not accepting gifts of money.

Life in the monastery

Monks and nuns live a very simple lifestyle. Typically, monks in a Theravada monastery get up early and have two meals – breakfast and lunch. After midday, they are only allowed water or tea. The monks' food is provided by local people who bring it to the monastery or invite the monks to their homes. During the day, time is set aside for meditation, studying the sacred texts, and conducting ceremonies and puja for laypeople. Traditionally, monks are also expected to teach, guide and counsel anyone who wishes to learn about the Dhamma or seeks their advice.

In a Zen monastery, life is very strict and strenuous. At the heart of the monastery is the *Zendo* or meditation hall, where the monks meditate, and where they sleep on mats on the floor. Their few possessions are kept in a small locker. They take their simple meals in silence, after special chanting in which all the monks join. During the day, the monks spend long hours in the *Sodo*, or monastery school, studying under their *roshis* (masters).

◄ *Monks in the Jokhang Temple in Lhasa, Tibet, read from the sacred texts. Studying the sacred texts is an important part of their daily lives.*

▲ Zen monks in a monastery in Japan, practising meditation. They spend many hours each day learning to meditate.

In our own words

"I am a fully ordained nun in the Karma Kagyu tradition of Tibetan Buddhism. There were two reasons why I felt I wanted to take this commitment for the rest of my life. The first was emotional: I had an overwhelming feeling that this was the only thing I wanted to do. Less immediate, but still relevant, was the rational understanding that becoming ordained was the best way to make life meaningful and to become more useful to others. This understanding built up gradually over several years, nurtured by the advice and good example of Tibetan lama-monks as well as a few Western monks and nuns. That was over 15 years ago and I have never regretted it. Life just gets better and better!"

Gelongma Konchok Lhamo, Kagyu Samye Ling Tibetan Centre, UK

weblinks

For more information about a Zen monastery, go to www.waylinks.co.uk/series/ 21stcentury/Buddhism

5 Buddhism and society

*I*n traditional Buddhist countries, such as Sri Lanka and Thailand, the Sangha has played, and continues to play, a very important role in society. Viharas and temples are often at the centre of village or town life, and are used as schools and community centres. While lay Buddhists have a duty to support their local monastery and its monks, the monks teach people about the Dhamma and help them to live life according to Buddhist principles.

Moral issues

For Buddhists, all moral issues are to be approached with the Five Moral Precepts and the teachings on wisdom, compassion, loving kindness and karma in mind. Although there are guidelines for how people should behave, it is up to each individual person to take responsibility for deciding what is right and what is wrong.

Animal welfare

The first of the Five Precepts is to undertake to avoid killing or harming any living thing, and to cultivate loving-kindness. Many Buddhists try to develop a loving appreciation for animals and nature, as well as other people. The Buddha taught that if people are training themselves to become more loving and kind, they need to use imagination. If they remember how it feels to suffer pain and fear, they will not wish to cause pain for others. The Buddha also taught that everything is dependent on other things, so all actions have consequences for the person doing them, and for other living things. (For example, when poison is used to kill slugs, it also kills the birds that eat slugs.) This has led some Buddhists to

◄ *In Asia, elephants such as this one have traditionally been used in the timber industry to haul logs from place to place.*

become deeply involved with environmental and ecological concerns.

In Myanmar, Buddhists and conservationists are working together to protect the country's endangered elephants. Elephants have been used in Asia for centuries for work, war, ceremonial and religious purposes. They often appear in Buddhist stories, such as the *Jatakas* (see page 22), as symbols of wisdom and strength. Today, Myanmar's elephants are seriously threatened by habitat loss and poaching. This has brought the elephants and local people increasingly into conflict. In this innovative project, Buddhists are helping conservationists to collect vital information about the elephants. Monks are also working with local people in many places to help them live in harmony with the elephants and to protect them.

Vegetarianism

To follow the First Precept, many Buddhists choose to be vegetarians. They do not eat meat because this involves killing a living thing. But the Buddhist teachings do not forbid people to eat meat, and in some countries, for example Tibet, meat is an important part of people's diets. Monks are expected to be grateful for whatever food people give them, including meat.

▼ *Monks receive gifts of food in Bangkok, Thailand. Local people hope to gain merit by giving food as alms. In return, the monks are grateful for whatever is put in their begging bowls. The monks take the food back to the monastery to eat.*

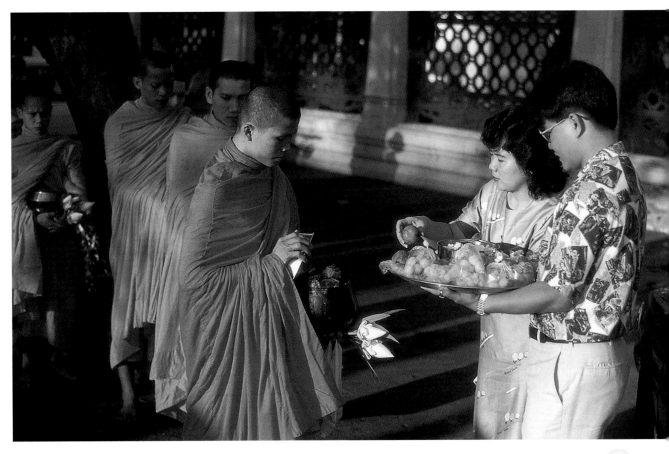

Engaged Buddhism

Apart from conservation, many Buddhists are becoming involved in what they call 'engaged Buddhism'. This means becoming more 'engaged' in social work – setting up hospitals, hospices and AIDS charities; in human rights – visiting prisoners for example; and in peace campaigning and politics (see page 42). Although 'engaged Buddhism' represents a new, and sometimes controversial, chapter in Buddhism's history, it is nonetheless rooted in ancient Buddhist teachings of mindfulness, compassion and loving kindness for all living beings.

▼ *A Tibetan monk and former political prisoner, Palden Gyatsu, leads a protest against British involvement in the international arms trade outside an arms fair in the UK in 1997.*

International network

The International Network of Engaged Buddhists (INEB) began in 1989 in Thailand. Since then, it has grown rapidly and now has members and runs projects in 33 countries. Its aim is to combine Buddhist practice with social action for a just and peaceful world. Non-Buddhists can join the INEB. They must simply be committed to helping others out of compassion. A key INEB activity is helping war-torn communities to resolve conflicts without using violence. This includes organising four annual Dharma Peace Walks in Cambodia.

---

weblinks

For information about another example of 'engaged Buddhism', go to
www.waylinks.co.uk/series/21stcentury/Buddhism

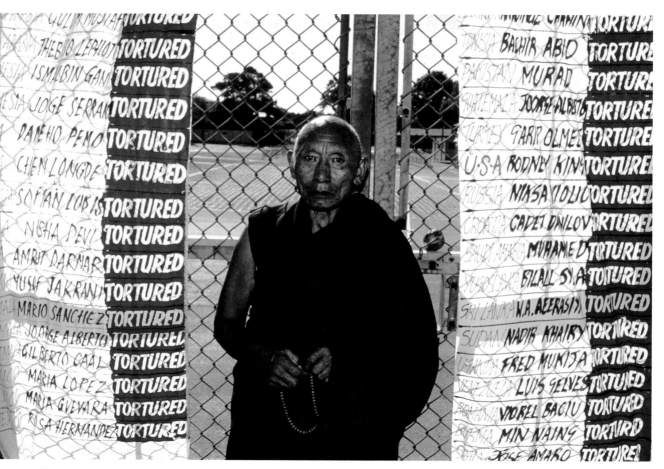

Drug rehabilitation

One example of 'engaged Buddhism' in action is the work of the Wat Tham Krabok, a monastery situated in the mountains of Thailand. For the last 50 years it has run a detoxification programme for drug addicts, based on Buddhist principles. Addicts mostly come from Thailand, but many Europeans and Australians have also visited the monastery. On arrival, they must take an oath, stating their commitment to the programme and to staying drug and alcohol-free for the rest of their lives. The programme itself is strict but highly successful. It involves drinking a special herbal mixture and taking herbal steam baths to get rid of toxins and cleanse the body. Monks and nuns are constantly on hand to supervise, and to offer counselling and support.

Prison visiting

The Angulimala Buddhist Prison Chaplaincy Organisation was set up in Britain in 1985 by an English Buddhist monk, Venerable Khemadhammo Mahathera. The organization is named after Angulimala, a notorious robber and murderer who was converted by the Buddha and became a monk. The story of Angulimala shows the principle on which the organization is based – that Enlightenment is possible in the most difficult circumstances, and that people can change. A team of Buddhist chaplains visits prisons to teach inmates about Buddhism, although prisoners do not have to be or become Buddhists.

▼ *Young drug addicts take part in a Buddhist ceremony in the Wat Tham Krabok monastery in Thailand.*

6 Current issues and world role

As it moves into the 21st century, Buddhism faces many challenges. For many traditional Buddhist countries, the 20th century proved a time of mixed fortunes. In countries such as China, Tibet and Myanmar, Buddhists faced and continue to face persecution under the Communist and military regimes. In other Asian countries, war, ethnic conflict and nationalist unrest put Buddhism under serious threat. And, as more countries have become Westernized and concerned with material wealth, the traditional values and teachings of Buddhism have been undermined. Nevertheless, in some places such as Indonesia and India, Buddhism has begun to re-establish its presence and win new support. Meanwhile, it continues to expand quickly in the 'new' territories of Europe, Australia and North America.

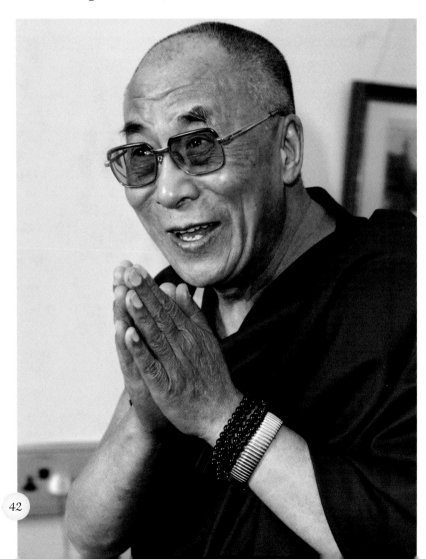

weblinks

For more information about Tibet and the Tibetan Government-in-Exile, go to www.waylinks.co.uk/series/21stcentury/Buddhism

◄ The Dalai Lama, the leader of Tibet's Buddhists, now lives in exile in Dharamsala, India. His title means 'a teacher whose wisdom is as deep as the ocean'.

Buddhism in exile

In 1951, Chinese Communists invaded Tibet. Until that time, the Dalai Lama had been Tibet's religious leader and head of its government. However, the Communist regime objected to religious practices. Hundreds of Buddhist monasteries were destroyed, thousands of monks imprisoned or killed, and the teaching and study of Buddhism was outlawed. In 1959, after an unsuccessful Tibetan uprising against the Chinese, the Dalai Lama fled to India where he now leads the Tibetans in exile. Many other monks and teachers also escaped, and they established a thriving Buddhist community in Dharamsala, India. Famous for his warmth, wisdom and compassion, and believed by Tibetans to be a living bodhisattva, the Dalai Lama travels all over the world, campaigning for the rights of the Tibetan people and suggesting non-violent solutions to his country's problems. In 1989, he was awarded the Nobel Peace Prize.

Buddhism in India

By the 12th century CE, Buddhism had almost disappeared from India and Hinduism and Islam became the country's major religions. Recently, however, Buddhism has enjoyed something of a revival in India, largely through the work of an Indian lawyer and politician, Dr B. R. Ambedkar (1891-1956). Born into a *Dalit* family, Ambedkar spent his life fighting for equal rights for Dalits, the lowest group in Indian Hindu society. Hostility from orthodox Hindus towards Ambedkar's demands led him to break away from Hinduism. In 1956, just before his death, he became a Buddhist and committed himself to the Buddhist principle of equality. Millions of Dalits followed his lead and the Ambedkar Buddhists have since become the largest single group of Buddhists in India.

▼ *Dr Ambedkar addresses a large crowd in India before a mass conversion to Buddhism in 1956.*

Buddhism in the West

Buddhism reached the West at the end of the 19th century, through the writings of Western scholars and their translations of Buddhist sacred texts. In 1881, the Pali Text Society was founded by a British scholar, T.W. Rhys Davids, while working for the Civil Service in Sri Lanka (then Ceylon). The Society collected, translated and published the sacred texts of Theravada Buddhism and made them available in Britain. At the same time, people from traditionally Buddhist countries in Asia began to settle in Europe and North America. Later, Westerners became interested and began to convert to Buddhism.

Friends of the Western Buddhist Order

The Friends of the Western Buddhist Order was started by an English Buddhist monk, Venerable Sangharakshita. He had studied many different branches of Buddhism and wanted to form a Buddhist movement which combined elements of many traditions. He also wanted the movement to be suited to Western society. For example, order members do not wear robes but have a *kesa* (scarf) for special ceremonies. Highly committed Buddhists are ordained as 'members' and take a new Buddhist name, but do not become monks or nuns. The Order is based in the United Kingdom.

New Buddhist movements

One of the fastest-growing of the new Buddhist groups in the West has been the Soka Gakkai, or 'Society for the Creation of Value'. It was founded in 1930 as an offshoot of the Nichiren school, based on the teachings of the Japanese monk, Nichiren (1222-83). It teaches chanting as a means not only to spiritual rewards but also to health, personal happiness and material gain. It set up centres in the USA in the 1960s, and in Europe in the 1970s and 1980s.

weblinks

For more information about the Friends of the Western Buddhist Order, go to
www.waylinks.co.uk/series/21stcentury/Buddhism

▼ *A member of the Western Buddhist Order honours the Buddha in a temple in Manchester, UK. He is wearing a kesa (scarf) around his neck.*

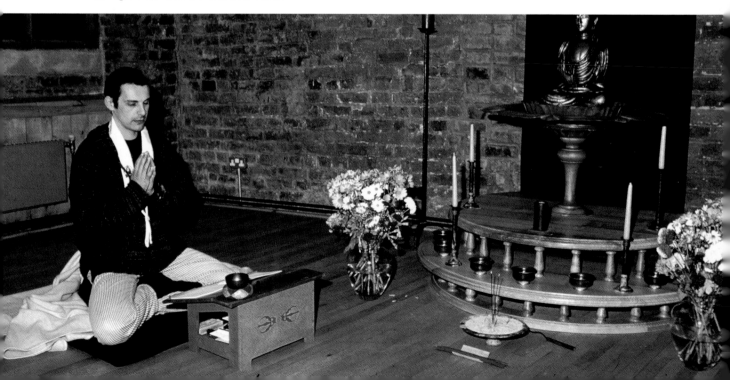

In our own words

The future of Western Buddhism

"I think Buddhism will continue growing in the West. Buddhism emphasizes loving kindness and says that each of us can change our own lives and the world by taking responsibility for the consequences of our actions. As people find greed more and more destructive to society and the environment, they may find Buddhism a very attractive and effective path.

We will continue to see three particular features in Western Buddhism:

1 *Women will be taken much more seriously than they have been traditionally.*

2 *The relationship between the monastic and lay Buddhist communities will change because Western laypeople are well-educated and may study, meditate and teach as much as monks or nuns.*

3 *Western Buddhists will become more and more socially and politically active."*

Munisha, Member of the Western Buddhist Order, UK

▼ *A Buddhist temple in Little Tokyo, Los Angeles, USA. In the 21st century, Buddhism is set to become more popular in countries beyond its original Asian homeland.*

weblinks

For more information about modern Buddhism, go to
www.waylinks.co.uk/series/21stcentury/Buddhism

Glossary

anatta (Sanskrit: *anatman*) The Pali word for no fixed self. Buddhists do not believe in a fixed soul or spirit which lives on after the body dies. They believe that everything is always changing.

anicca (Sanskrit: *anitya*) The Pali word for the Buddhist belief in impermanence, that is that nothing lasts for ever but is always changing.

arahat (Sanskrit: *arhat*) The Pali word for an Enlightened person who is on the highest stage leading to nirvana and whose mind is free from hatred, ignorance and greed.

bhikkhu (Sanskrit: *bhikshu*) The Pali word for a Buddhist monk.

bhikkhuni (Sanskrit: *bhikshuni*) The Pali word for a Buddhist nun.

bodhi tree The fig tree under which the Buddha is believed to have gained Enlightenment.

bodhisattva A mythical, heroic figure in Mahayana Buddhism who has gained Enlightenment and become a Buddha. Out of compassion for the world, the bodhisattva chooses to help other people overcome their suffering.

caste The classes or divisions in Hindu society.

Dalits Members of the lowest rank of Hindu society, previously known as 'untouchables'. The word Dalit means 'oppressed'.

Dhamma (Sanskrit: *Dharma*) The Pali word for the Buddha's teaching.

dukkha (Sanskrit: *duhka*) The Pali word for suffering.

Enlightenment The experience of understanding the truth about the world and how things really are.

karma (Pali: *kamma*) The Sanskrit word for the good and bad actions that affect a person's position in this and future lives.

kesa A scarf worn by members of the Friends of the Western Buddhist Order for special ceremonies.

Mahayana One of the two main schools of Buddhism. It means 'the great way'.

mandala A circular picture that Tibetan Buddhists use to help them meditate. In their minds, they follow a path into the centre of the picture, like following a map.

meditation A central part of Buddhist practice, the goal of meditation is to quiet or still the mind in order to experience inner peace.

metta (Sanskrit: *maitri*) The Pali word for the key Buddhist virtue of loving kindness and generosity to others, without thought of reward.

mudra (Pali: *mudda*) The Sanskrit word for symbolic shapes made by the hands in images of the Buddha and bodhisattvas. Each mudra has a special meaning.

Mughal The Muslim rulers of India from 1526-1857.

nirvana (Pali: *nibbana*) The perfect peace and happiness entered when the cycle of birth and rebirth is broken and suffering ends.

pagoda A style of stupa found in China, Japan and parts of Southeast Asia.

Pali An ancient Indian language in which the texts of the Theravada Buddhists were first written down.

parinirvana (Pali: *parinibbana*) The Sanskrit word for the final and complete nirvana reached when the Buddha passed away.

puja The name given to a ceremony of devotion and worship in Buddhism and Hinduism.

Sangha The community of Buddhists, which began with the Buddha's first followers. For some Buddhists, the sangha particularly means monks and nuns. For others, it includes all Buddhists.

Sanskrit An ancient Indian language in which many Mahayana sacred texts are written down. It is a sacred language for Hindus.

Silk Road An ancient overland route between Europe and Asia, along which goods such as silk, and later, ideas and religions, were carried.

skandha (Pali: *khandha*) The Sanskrit word for each of the five parts or elements that make up a human being. They way these five parts come together changes with each rebirth.

stupa A dome-shaped Buddhist monument.

sutra (Pali: *sutta*) The Sanskrit word for a short Buddhist sacred text.

Tantric A form of Buddhism from Tibet, based on mysterious texts describing rituals, magic and meditation techniques.

Theravada One of the two main schools of Buddhism. It means 'way of the elders'.

Tipitaka (Sanskrit: *Tripitaka*) The Pali word for the sacred texts of the Theravada Buddhists. Also known as the *Pali Canon*.

vihara A Buddhist monastery or temple.

vinaya The rules of discipline for Buddhist monks and nuns.

Zen A school of Mahayana Buddhism from China and Japan. The word Zen means 'meditation'.

Timeline

c.623 BCE	Siddhattha Gotama born in Lumbini, Nepal
c.588 BCE	Siddhattha gains Enlightenment in Bodh Gaya, India, and becomes the Buddha
c.543 BCE	The Buddha passes away in Kushinagara, India
c.543-443 BCE	Two councils held to collect the Buddha's teachings together. Buddhism splits into the Theravada and Mahayana schools
268-239 BCE	Reign of Emperor Ashoka Maurya in India. Buddhism becomes the major faith of India
c.250 BCE	Buddhism reaches Sri Lanka and later, Myanmar
1st century BCE	*Tipitaka (Pali Canon)* is written down
1st century CE	Buddhism reaches China. First images of the Buddha made
4th century CE	Buddhism reaches Korea
7th century CE	Buddhism reaches Tibet
6th century CE	Buddhism reaches Japan
12th century CE	Buddhism almost disappears from India. Zen Buddhism reaches Japan from China
13th century CE	Buddhism the official religion in Thailand, Cambodia and Laos
1881	Pali Text Society founded to translate Pali texts into English
1891	Mahabodhi Society founded in Sri Lanka to unite Buddhists and raise funds to restore sacred Buddhist sites in India
1907	First Buddhist Society in Britain formed
1930	Buddhist Society of America formed
1935	The present Dalai Lama born in Tibet
1956	In India, Dr Ambedkar converts many people to Buddhism
1967	Friends of the Western Buddhist Order founded in the UK
1989	Dalai Lama receives the Nobel Peace Prize
1989	International Network of Engaged Buddhists begins in Thailand

Further reading

Teach Yourself Buddhism by Clive Erricker (Hodder Headline PLC, 1995)

Buddha for Beginners by Jane Hope and Borin Van Loon (Icon Books, 1994)

World Religions: Buddhism by Holly Connolly and Peter Connolly (Stanley Thornes Ltd, 1992)

The Dhammapada, translated by Juan Mascaro (Penguin Classics, 1973)

Before He Was the Buddha by Hammalawa Saddhatissa (Seastone, Ulysses Press, 1998)

Index